Little People, **BIG DREAMS**

DOLLY PARTON

Written by
Mª Isabel Sánchez Vegara

Illustrated by
Daria Solak

Frances Lincoln
Children's Books

Little Dolly grew up in the foothills of Tennessee's Great Smoky Mountains, with her 11 siblings. She didn't have much, but she was gifted with a lovely voice— and that was worth more than any treasure.

She began to write songs on her guitar and perform them for whoever would listen. Singing barefoot on the front porch, Dolly dreamed of jumping onstage in high heels.

Her uncle Bill was amazed by her talent and helped her to get started in the music business.

Dolly was just 10 years old when she got a regular slot singing for a radio station, fitting it in alongside school.

When Dolly graduated from school, she moved to Nashville, the city of music. With her soulful voice and songwriting talent, she was ready to become a star.

One day, standing outside a laundromat, Dolly met
a young man named Carl, and they instantly fell in love.
He became her anchor, and she, his never-ending excitement.

But music was still her greatest love. So when Porter Wagoner—a famous country entertainer—asked Dolly to sing with him, she didn't have to think twice.

Dolly topped the charts with Porter. But she also wrote many moving songs on the trials of being a woman, and earned herself loyal fans. It was time for her to go solo.

She became the most popular singer on the country music scene. But she dreamed of making as many people happy as she could, so she started to look for new adventures.

Dolly crossed over into pop music and sang with the most amazing artists of her time, like Kenny Rogers.

With her unique voice and fabulous image, she became a total superstar.

She loved wearing wigs and lots of makeup. Maybe some people thought it was too much, but children loved her look and she did, too.

Dolly decided to do something great for the children who loved her, and started a special library that would send books to kids in need: from her hometown to the other side of the world.

But Dolly didn't stop there. She built a theme park and became the most successful woman in show business. She now owns radio stations, TV channels, and record companies, too.

And after 50 years onstage, little Dolly has become
the most respected country performer of all time.
A larger-than-life living legend, with a heart
as big as her dreams.

DOLLY PARTON

(Born 1946)

1955

1976

Dolly Parton grew up near the Great Smoky Mountains, in East Tennessee. Her family didn't have much money, but thanks to her mother's love and her musical talent, she felt rich in other ways. Singing was like breathing in her family. Her uncle Lewis gave her a guitar, and her uncle Bill helped her to get started in the music business. She sang on local radio and television and started recording with a music label at age 13. A day after graduating high school, Dolly moved to Nashville, the home of country music. She then met her future husband, Carl Dean, the day after that! Dolly got her big musical break at the age of 19, singing with Porter Wagoner on *The Porter Wagoner Show*. They worked as a creative duo for eight years, before Dolly decided to go solo. Ultimately, this turned out to be a great decision. Dolly